SOCCER CHAMPIONS

BY JIM WHITING

FC BARCELONA

Published by Creative Education
and Creative Paperbacks
P.O. Box 227, Mankato, Minnesota 56002
Creative Education and Creative Paperbacks
are imprints of The Creative Company
www.thecreativecompany.us

Design and production by The Design Lab
Art direction by Rita Marshall
Printed in Malaysia

Photographs by Alamy (MARKA), Corbis (Matthew Ashton/
AMA/AMA, Colorsport, Corbis, Hulton-Deutsch Collection/
CORBIS, JUAN MEDINA/Reuters, Gustau Nacarino/
Reuters, Daniel Ochoa De Olza/AP, GERRY PENNY/
epa, Dan Rowley/Colorsport), Getty Images (STAFF, Bob
Thomas, Bob Thomas/Popperfoto), photosinbox.com,
Shutterstock (gualtiero boffi, Boris15, catwalker, CHEN
WS, Denis Kuvaev, Marzolino, Maxisport, mooinblack,
Natursports), Wikimedia Creative Commons (A.A. Artis,
Mutari, Nationaal Archief/Den Haag/Rijksfotoarchief:
Fotocollectie Algemeen Nederlands Fotopersbureau
[ANEFO], Núria, Pot, Harry/Anefo, Tot-futbol, Unknown)

Library of Congress Cataloging-in-Publication Data
Whiting, Jim.
FC Barcelona / by Jim Whiting.
p. cm. — (Soccer champions)
Includes bibliographical references and index.
Summary: A chronicle of the people, matches,
and world events that shaped the European men's
Spanish soccer team known as FC Barcelona,
from its founding in 1899 to today.
ISBN 978-1-60818-586-3 (hardcover)
ISBN 978-1-62832-191-3 (pbk)
1. Fútbol Club Barcelona—History—
Juvenile literature. I. Title.

GV943.6.B3W45 2015
796.334'64094672—dc23   2014029643

CCSS: RI.5.1, 2, 3, 8; RH.6-8.4, 5, 7

First Edition HC 9 8 7 6 5 4 3 2 1
First Edition PBK 9 8 7 6 5 4 3 2 1

Cover and page 3: Defender Jordi Alba
(#18) and forward Lionel Messi (#10)
Page 1: 2011 Supercopa de España final

TABLE OF

Midfielder Alexis Sánchez

INTRODUCTION

Soccer (or football, as it is known almost everywhere else in the world) is truly a universal game. Nowhere is the play more competitive than in Europe. Almost every European country has its own league, and generally that league has several divisions. A typical season lasts eight or nine months, from late summer to mid-spring. Every team in each level plays all other teams in its level twice, once at home and once on the other team's pitch. At the end of the season, the bottommost teams in one division are relegated (moved down) to the next lower division, with the same number of topmost teams from that lower division promoted to replace them. Such a system ensures that a high level of competition is maintained and that late-season games between teams with losing records remain important as they seek to avoid relegation.

Individual countries also feature their own tournaments, such as England's FA Cup and Spain's Copa del Rey. In theory, these tournaments allow almost any team the opportunity to win the championship, but in reality the best clubs dominate the competition. An assortment of European-wide tournaments complement individual nations' league and cup play. The most prestigious is the Union of European Football Associations (UEFA) Champions League. Known as the European Cup until

Spain's FC Barcelona has proven itself to be one of the world's most competitive football clubs.

1993, the Champions League is a tournament consisting of 32 teams drawn primarily from the highest finishers in the strongest national leagues. Other teams can play their way into the tournament in preliminary rounds. It originated in 1954, when the otherwise obscure Wolverhampton Wanderers of England defeated Honved, the top-rated Hungarian side, prompting Wanderers manager Stan Cullis to declare his team "Champions of the World." Noted French soccer journalist Gabriel Hanot disagreed and helped organize a continent-wide competition that began in 1956.

The Champions League starts with eight four-team pools, which play two games with one another. The top two teams from each pool begin a series of knockout rounds, also contested on a two-game basis. The last two teams play a single championship game at a neutral site. The tournament runs concurrently with league play, beginning in September and concluding in May. Teams that win their league, their national cup, and the Champions League during the same season are said to have won the Continental Treble—almost certainly the most difficult feat in all of professional sports. The winner of the Champions League is eligible for the FIFA Club World Cup, an annual seven-team tournament that originated in 2000. It also includes teams from the Americas and Caribbean, Africa, Asia, Oceania, and the host nation.

The other major European club championship is the UEFA Europa League, founded in 1971 and known as the UEFA Cup until the 2009–10 season. The winners of these two tournaments play for the UEFA Super Cup, usually held in August.

ALL-TIME CHAMPIONS LEAGUE RECORDS OF THE TOP 10 CLUBS (AS OF 2014):

	Winner	Runner-up
Real Madrid (Spain)	10	3
AC Milan (Italy)	7	4
Bayern Munich (Germany)	5	5
Liverpool (England)	5	2
Barcelona (Spain)	4	3
Ajax (Netherlands)	4	2
Manchester United (England)	3	2
Inter Milan (Italy)	3	2
Benfica (Portugal)	2	5
Juventus (Italy)	2	5

Camp Nou stadium

CONTINENTAL TREBLE WINNERS

Celtic (Scotland)	1966–67
Ajax (Netherlands)	1971–72
PSV (Netherlands)	1987–88
Manchester United (England)	1998–99
Barcelona (Spain)	2008–09
Inter Milan (Italy)	2009–10
Bayern Munich (Germany)	2012–13

A MUTUAL UNADMIRATION SOCIETY

The Barcelona harbor, located at the base of Montjuïc hill, became a key port for international trade.

The origins of Barcelona, Spain, are shrouded in myth. According to legend, the city was founded by Carthaginian general Hamilcar Barca in the third century B.C. and named for him. Eventually, it became an important Roman city and then the capital of Catalonia, a Spanish region with its own language, government, and set of traditions. Today, Barcelona is the second-largest city in Spain, especially noted for its architecture and culture. In addition, Barcelona has a strong tradition in sports, reflected in its selection to host the 1992 Summer Olympics. This sporting tradition extends to soccer. FC Barcelona, familiarly known as Barça (*BAHR-suh*), has an immense worldwide fan base. It is the only soccer club in the world that also encompasses teams in basketball, handball, ice hockey, roller hockey, futsal (a form of indoor soccer with five players on a side), and rugby.

The origins of this colossus couldn't have been more humble. On October 22, 1899, Hans Kamper, a 22-year-old Swiss businessman living in Barcelona, ran an announcement in the newspaper *Los Deportes*:

> Our friend and companion Hans Kamper … former Swiss [football] champion, being keen on organizing some football games in the city, asks anyone who feels enthusiastic enough about the sport to present themselves at the offices of this newspaper any Tuesday or Friday evening between the hours of 9 and 11 P.M.

Eleven young men—two other Swiss, two Englishmen, a German, and half a dozen Catalans—responded. They named their new team Fùtbol Club (FC) Barcelona. The first members also chose FC Barcelona's enduring colors: blue and maroon, giving rise to the team's nickname of "Blaugrana" (blue/deep red).

Their timing was ideal. Spain had been crushed by the United States in the Spanish–American War in 1898, losing the final remnants of an empire that a few centuries earlier had been one of the world's richest and most powerful.

What was bad for Spain was good for Catalonia. "Barcelona became one of the most vibrant and wealthiest cities in Europe," said Irish actor and political activist Ardal O'Hanlon. "FC Barcelona was a crucial part of Catalonia's newfound optimism and prosperity." This prosperity led to more leisure time and a corresponding interest in sports. The citizens of Barcelona quickly embraced the new team, and the

King Philip V's accession to the throne helped trigger
the War of the Spanish Succession (1701–14).

team embraced the city—even adopting Barcelona's official coat of arms as its own.
Eventually, the founder changed his name to Joan Gamper, its Catalan equivalent.

From the start, the team lived up to what would later become its official motto:
"*Més que un club*" (More than a club). FC Barcelona became the symbolic standard-
bearer for Catalan traditions, which often differed from the rest of Spain—in
particular Madrid, the Spanish capital. Unlike most sports rivalries, this one is
grounded in history. Many historians date it to 1714, when forces loyal to Spanish
King Philip V conquered Barcelona after a lengthy siege. The date of the city's fall,
September 11, is observed as the National Day of Catalonia. As soccer writer Sid
Lowe observes, "The *diada* [September 11] 'celebrates' defeat … and reinforces the
idea of Madrid as the natural enemy."

This antagonism carries over onto the pitch. Games with Real Madrid, a team

Today, many citizens of Catalonia make an effort to distance themselves from a Spanish identity.

whose location in the capital makes it stand for everything Catalans detest about the central government, are arguably the most heated in soccer, if not the entire sports world. Because both teams are members of La Liga, the top Spanish league, they are guaranteed to meet at least twice every season. These games are referred to as El Clásico (the classic). Few Spanish soccer fans are indifferent about the outcome.

When Barcelona hosts El Clásico, huge banners proclaiming that "Catalonia is Not Spain" festoon the stands. As the clock ticks up to 17:14 (the year of the Barcelona siege), Barcelona supporters chant, "Independence! Independence! Independence!" Soccer isn't the only sport affected by the Catalonia-Spain rivalry, and sometimes fans become especially cruel. In 1989, a Real Madrid basketball player's brother was killed in a car crash. When Barça hosted Madrid soon afterward, fans chanted, "Where is your brother?" every time the unfortunate player touched the ball.

THE GOLDEN AGE

*During Alfonso XIII's reign (1886–1931), Spain
sustained political instability and power shifts.*

The first El Clásico was in 1902, in a hastily assembled competition called the Copa de la Coronación (Coronation Cup) to honor the accession of 16-year-old Alfonso XIII as the new Spanish monarch. Barcelona defeated the newly formed Madrid FC 3–1. The teams didn't meet again for four years. Barça won that game as well, 5–2.

In its first years as a club, Barcelona worked to establish a successful roster and bolster its weak finances.

With the club struggling financially in 1908, Gamper became president and kept it going with his own money. The club membership increased nearly 15-fold, from 201 in 1909 to 2,973 in less than 10 years. This growth was helped by FC Barcelona's first formal facility, Carrer de la Indústria, for which Gamper helped raise funds. The towering 2-tier seating area—the first of its kind in Spain—held 6,000 spectators.

By then, the Coronation Cup had become the Copa del Rey (King's Cup), a tournament that was the country's first nationwide competition. Barça began a sustained run of success in 1910, winning the Copa del Rey and the first of four straight Pyrenees Cups (an early international competition). Prolific goal-scoring forward Paulino Alcántara emerged during this time.

In 1919, the team began what many fans refer to as the "golden age." Between then and 1928, the team won the Copa del Rey five times. It also dominated play in the Campionat de Catalunya, a Catalan regional league. A key player was Josep "Pepe" Samitier, who joined the team at the age of 17. Initially a defender, Samitier became a terror all over the field. The other big star was goalkeeper Ricardo Zamora, especially noted for his game apparel: a tweed cap in homage to the sport's English pioneers and a white polo beneath a sweater. His successor Ferenc Platko was just as good. Forward Emili Sagi, winger Vicenç Piera, and powerful midfielder Agustí Sancho also played key roles.

In 1922, the team's success resulted in a larger home, Camp de Les Corts, which seated 22,000 fans. Three years later, Barça witnessed a sign of the politics that would tear the country apart in little more than a decade. When the Barcelona crowd jeered the Spanish national anthem before a home game, Spanish dictator Miguel Primo de Rivera closed down the club for several months in addition to stripping Gamper of his presidency.

Barça's golden era was capped in 1929 when it won the first season of the national soccer league, La Liga, edging Madrid by two points. By then, King Alfonso had allowed Madrid and several other teams to add the word *real* (ray-ALL), meaning "royal," to their names. When he didn't extend that privilege to Barcelona, the snub served only to increase the intensity of the rivalry with Madrid. At that point, the matches had become decidedly one-sided. Barça had won 17 times and Madrid only 3, with another 7 ending in ties.

EMERGING FROM CHAOS

Though Barça continued to win Catalan championships, the team enjoyed little success on the national level. This decline was accompanied by increasingly ominous political developments, which flared into a full-scale civil war in 1936. Generalissimo Francisco Franco organized an uprising against a government that had been elected five years earlier and established as the Second Spanish Republic. Franco and his followers branded themselves as Nationalists and fought the defenders of the Republic, known as Republicans. It was an especially brutal conflict, with mass executions common on both sides.

Some leading soccer figures nearly became casualties. Though Catalonia was firmly on the Republican side, Alcántara was placed on a Republican death list because of his supposed pro-Franco views. He fled to safety in France. Others weren't so lucky. The dead included Ángel Arocha, a prolific Barça striker who averaged more than a goal a game in upwards of 200 appearances. Especially tragic was the loss of Barça president Josep Sunyol soon after the war began. After visiting a group of Catalan troops, he strayed into Nationalist territory and was executed.

Soccer continued on, though at a reduced level. When the war canceled

Franco (opposite) faced heavy opposition from revolutionary groups based in Barcelona.

La Liga play, a small number of teams from Catalonia and Valencia competed in the newly organized Mediterranean League for the 1936–37 season, with Barça coming out the winner. Franco abolished the organization in 1939 when the Nationalists emerged victorious and he became the dictator of Spain.

That was the start of Barça's struggles. Franco ordered the club's coat of arms to be changed because it wasn't "Spanish" enough. Some players were suspended or exiled. He forbade people from speaking in Catalan and displaying the senyera, the Catalan flag. In 1943, the team bottomed out, suffering an 11–1 drubbing by Real Madrid as Franco officials and a frenzied crowd intimidated the team.

Despite the difficulties, the team slowly emerged from the chaos. Players such as forward César Rodríguez, who scored 294 goals in 433 games, and forward Mariano Martín played key roles.

So did winger Estanislau Basora and keeper Antoni Ramallets, who inspired comparisons with the keeper legends of the 1920s. Samitier returned as manager and led the team to the 1944–45 La Liga title, its first since the league's inaugural season. In 1949, the team hoisted the Latin Cup. A precursor to the European Cup, the tournament included teams from France, Italy, Portugal, and Spain.

In 1951, the club made one of the most important moves in its history, adding Hungarian forward László Kubala. He was renowned for his passing and dribbling skills in addition to his goal-scoring prowess. He was also regarded as one of soccer's all-time best penalty kickers with his ability to curve the ball. A fan poll in 1999 proclaimed Kubala as Barça's best-ever player.

With Kubala—who once scored seven goals in a single game—joining

an already gifted roster, Barça's 1951–52 season was one of the greatest in soccer history. The "Five-Cup Team" won La Liga, Copa del Rey, Latin Cup, Copa Eva Duarte (matching La Liga and Copa del Rey winners and awarded to Barça for capturing both titles), and the Copa Martini Rossi (featuring several top European clubs). 1n 1953, the team narrowly missed signing Argentine superstar Alfredo Di Stéfano. In a controversial situation in which many people believe Franco became personally involved, Di Stéfano wound up with Real Madrid, adding even more fuel to the Spanish teams' rivalry when he became Europe's most dominant player. Barça received some solace when forward Luis Suárez arrived in 1954. He became known as "El Arquitecto" (The Architect) for his creativity in constructing scoring opportunities. Barça fans were labeled as either *kubalistes* (fans of Kubala) or *suaristes* (fans of Suárez) as they—mostly good-naturedly—debated which player was better.

Kubala (opposite) and Suárez (above) helped Barça to international titles.

BARCELONA GETS A DUTCH TREAT—TWICE

It had long been apparent that the team had outgrown Les Corts. So in 1957, Barça began playing at Camp Nou, Europe's largest stadium with room for 93,000 spectators. Fittingly, Barça won the first game there, 4–2 against a team from Warsaw, Poland, with forward Eulogio Martínez scoring the facility's first-ever goal. The team continued to perform at a high level in 1958 when Helenio Herrera became manager

In 2014, FC Barcelona announced plans to renovate Camp Nou by 2021 and increase the already massive stadium's capacity.

and the team added still more talent, such as Hungarian forwards Sándor Kocsis and Zoltán Czibor. In 1958–59, the team had a double (which meant it won two major titles), taking La Liga and Copa del Rey crowns. The following season, Barcelona defended its La Liga championship, while Suárez became the only Spanish-born player to win the European Footballer of the Year award.

Despite all its accomplishments, Barça had been somewhat eclipsed when Real Madrid won the first-ever European Cup in 1956 and defended the title in four successive seasons. So it was a major milestone when the Blaugrana defeated Madrid early in the 1961 tournament and played Benfica of Portugal in the final. Kocsis opened the scoring with a header. Moments after tying the score, Benfica took the lead when Barça keeper Ramallets tipped a shot into the crossbar and it fell into the goal. The Portuguese took a 3–1 lead early in the second half. Czibor's goal with 15

Barcelona defeated Germany's Hamburg in the 1961 European Cup semifinals on its way to the final against Benfica.

Johan Cruyff (front row, center) and his teammates reestablished Barça as a top contender.

minutes left narrowed the margin to 3–2, but Benfica held on for the win. The loss marked the start of a long period of relative decline for Barça.

The team wasn't bad, with La Liga finishes ranging from second to sixth. The problem was that Real Madrid was better, winning 9 of the next 13 La Liga titles and adding a sixth European Cup, while Barça still had just one finals appearance to its name. The stars of the 1950s were also moving on. One of the few highlights of the era came in 1968, when Barça defeated Real in the Copa del Rey final 1–0. The win was all the more remarkable because it was played in Madrid. It became known as the "bottle final," a reference to Madrid fans who hurled dozens of glass bottles at Barça players in the game's waning moments.

Barça's fortunes took a turn in 1973 with the signing of Dutch superstar Johan Cruyff. "With Cruyff, everything changed—the club as well as the team," said teammate Juan Manuel Asensi. Barça won its first La Liga title in 14 years, thanks in part to Cruyff.

Five years later, Barça won the European Cup Winners' Cup, defeating Germany's Fortuna Düsseldorf. Fans were especially impressed with central defender Migueli, who played the final with a broken collarbone and went on to make 553 appearances for the club, a record that stood for 22 years. One of the biggest names ever to play for

Barça came on board during the 1980s: attacking midfielder Diego Maradona, the Argentine superstar who is counted among the greatest soccer players of all time. Though he helped Barça win the 1983 Copa del Ray—defeating Real Madrid in the final—and the Supercopa de España (matching La Liga and Copa del Rey winners), Maradona frequently clashed with team management and left after two seasons.

Barça finally made its second European Cup finals appearance in 1986, facing Steaua Bucureşti of Romania. Riding the momentum of the team's first La Liga title in 11 years, Barça had the advantage of what was almost a home pitch, since the game was in Seville, Spain. A win seemed almost a foregone conclusion, and the team booked a hotel ballroom in advance for a post-game victory dinner. But neither team scored in regulation, so the game went to a shootout. Steaua goalkeeper Helmuth Duckadam became the "Hero of Seville" by saving all four Barça shots, while his teammates scored twice in four attempts. "By not winning the European Cup, we threw mud over the league title," said one frustrated Barça player. The "victory dinner" was not a happy occasion.

The outlook improved two years later when Cruyff became manager and fashioned a roster that became known as the "Dream Team." The Catalan heart of the team was exemplified by midfielder Pep Guardiola, who conducted interviews in Catalan with a senyera nearby. He was joined by outstanding foreign players such as forward Hristo Stoichkov of Bulgaria, midfielder Ronald Koeman of the Netherlands, and midfielder Michael Laudrup of Denmark. Cruyff departed after the 1995–96 season as Barça's most successful manager, with the team's long-sought first European Cup and 10 other major trophies to his credit. Meanwhile, Barça also benefited from some good fortune. The club won La Liga three times on the final day of the season, thanks to losses suffered by its closest rivals.

Defender José Ramón Alexanko (front) attacked the Bucureşti goal in the 1986 European Cup final.

THE MESSI ERA

Xavi Hernández (left) teamed with Carles Puyol to take on Robinho and other top scorers during El Clásico matches.

Barça barely missed a beat when Cruyff moved on, notching its first La Liga/Copa del Rey double in 39 years in 1997–98, then adding another La Liga title in the following season—a fitting way of marking the club's 100th anniversary year. That would, however, be Barça's last major trophy for six seasons, its longest-ever dry spell. But several important players joined the team during this time, such as midfielder Xavi Hernández and central midfielder Andrés Iniesta. They joined defender Carles Puyol, a fixture in the lineup since Cruyff's final season as coach.

The infusion of talent paid off with the 2004–05 La Liga crown. That season also marked the debut of Lionel Messi, the Argentine forward who eventually would be favorably compared with his fabled countryman Diego Maradona. Barça defended its La Liga title the following season, then it faced Arsenal of England in the Champions League final. Barça was the favorite because of dominant players such as forward Ronaldinho and striker Samuel Eto'o, though Arsenal hadn't yielded a goal in its last 10 games leading up to the final. The Blaugrana spotted their rivals a goal near the end of the first half. Even playing a man up after an Arsenal player was sent off the pitch, Barça couldn't capitalize, missing a number of opportunities. Eto'o finally broke through in the 76th minute when he punched in the equalizer. Defender Juliano Belletti, who had just entered the game, scored the game-winner five minutes later.

Striker Henrik Larsson, Puyol, midfielder Deco, and Ronaldinho (front row) celebrated their Champions League win.

Messi and forward Thierry Henry helped lead the 2008–09 Blaugrana to a history-making season.

Although Messi emerged as one of the world's premier players, Barça slipped
slightly the two following seasons. But once again, hiring a former star player for
coaching duties produced big dividends, as Pep Guardiola took over for the 2008–09
season. Barça became the first Spanish team to win the Continental Treble, defeating
defending champion Manchester United 2–0 to take the Champions League title
shortly after winning both La Liga and the Copa del Rey. That set the stage for the
first-ever sextuple—winning six major championships in a calendar year—as Barça
also added the Supercopa de España, UEFA Super Cup, and FIFA Club World Cup.

In 2010, Italy's Inter Milan defeated Barça in the Champions League semifinals en route to claiming the cup. Barça returned to the finals the following year to win the title with a 3–1 triumph over Manchester United as winger Pedro Rodríguez, Messi, and striker David Villa scored. The club made the semifinals in 2012, losing to Chelsea. The Blaugrana had a chance for redemption the following year, once again advancing to the semis, but they were crushed 7–0 by eventual champion Bayern Munich of Germany.

Despite the loss to Bayern, four consecutive appearances in the finals or semifinals was the best streak in Cup history since Real Madrid had won the first five Cups in the 1950s. Messi was one of the primary reasons for this sustained excellence. He won four consecutive FIFA Ballon d'Or awards. In 2012, his 73 goals established a new mark for a European club season. That same year, Messi became the first player to score five goals in a single Champions League match. And in 2014, he became Barça's all-time leading scorer. The club rewarded him with a new contract that made him the world's highest-paid soccer player.

According to the team's lofty standards, the 2013–14 season represented a stumble, as the Blaugrana didn't win any major trophies for the first time since 2008. They lost in the Champions League quarterfinals and suffered defeat at the hands of Real Madrid in the Copa del Rey final. Having spent virtually the entire La Liga season clumped with Real and Atlético de Madrid at the top of the standings, Barça hoped to break away in the final game as it hosted Atlético. In a brutal match that included nine yellow cards and three players forced out by injury, Barça's first-half lead disappeared, and it tied with Real for second place in La Liga. "An unrepeatable era has come to an end," said defender Javier Mascherano. "Not in this club nor in any other will we again see what we have been through in these five or six years."

Nevertheless, the Blaugrana's ability to add young talent seemed likely to keep them in the upper ranks of European soccer. With Messi sidelined with injuries during part of the

In 2012, Messi's (above) record-breaking year earned him legions of fans (opposite).

Explosive Brazilian forward Neymar joined Barcelona in 2013, specializing in playmaking.

2013–14 season, newly acquired winger Neymar stepped up. The young Brazilian gave an early demonstration of his skills by scoring a hat trick in December. He was also named the world's most marketable athlete by *SportsPro* magazine. "He's everything a brand would want in an endorser, and all the signs are his career has not even peaked yet," said *SportsPro*'s editor-in-chief David Cushnan. Barça fans were also excited about speedy winger Adama Traoré, who joined the club at the age of eight and made his senior team debut in 2013.

While Madrid held the lead in La Liga titles as of 2014, with 32 to Barça's 22, Barça maintained the edge in Copa del Rey crowns (26 versus 19). Catalans took pride not only in Barça's trophies but also in the team's representation of the region to the rest of the world. As El Clásico seemed destined to retain its status as the most intense athletic competition in the world, Barça's fans planned to cheer on their favorite team's quest for excellence.

MEMORABLE MATCHES

1899

Team was founded.

1906

FC Barcelona v. Madrid

May 13, 1906, Barcelona, Spain

Facing Madrid for the first time in four years and just the second time overall, Barcelona dominated the action in a 5–2 win. Forward Charles Wallace and midfielder Francisco Sanz scored twice for the Blaugrana, with forward Romà Forns adding the fifth. According to a contemporary account, the seeds for the teams' bitter rivalry may have been sown that evening, when the winners hosted their opponents at Barcelona's elegant Francia restaurant. The Madrid players launched into a stream of complaints about the biased refereeing, the lack of sportsmanship on the part of the Barcelona players, and even some of the nasty things that the home crowd had yelled at them. As soccer authority Phil Ball observes, "It might not be going too far to say that the strife and struggles between the two clubs from 1905 onward accurately mirror the very essence of 20th-century Spanish history. The two cities have always been moving in different directions, partly through [stubbornness], partly through political allegiance, but mainly through clear cultural differences."

1958

FC Barcelona v. Real Madrid
El Clásico, October 26, 1958, Barcelona, Spain

The capacity crowd packing Camp Nou expected a tight match as the two rivals confronted each other early in the 1958–59 La Liga season. Real Madrid was undefeated, with Barça not far behind. Barça drew first blood, with forward Evaristo de Macedo converting a pass from forward Justo Tejada to take a 1–0 lead at halftime. Midway through the second half, de Macedo snaked his way through the Real defense for his second goal. Three minutes later, he completed a hat trick. A brawl broke out on the pitch soon afterward, and several players were ejected. Tejada rounded out the scoring with a solo run in the waning minutes. "I expected this 4–0 win," gloated manager Helenio Herrera in the locker room after the match. "I was convinced we'd thrash Real Madrid, because I know the class, fitness, and morale of my players." Herrera proved to be a prophet. His team went on to win La Liga by four points and also took the Copa del Rey to complete one of its most famous doubles.

1974

FC Barcelona v. Real Madrid
El Clásico, February 19, 1974, Madrid, Spain

Johan Cruyff's energy and influence on his new teammates were especially evident when the club traveled to Madrid. A scoreless tie on their home turf of Camp Nou in October 1973 had made the Blaugrana hungry for a win. Midfielder Juan Manuel Asensi opened the scoring at the half-hour mark, and Cruyff doubled the margin four minutes later. Asensi tallied again less than 10 minutes into the second half, then midfielder Juan Carlos and striker Hugo Sotil hit the back of the net within 4 minutes of each other to complete Barça's most decisive victory in the capital city. The normally boisterous Madrid crowd grew so quiet that Barça winger Carles Rexach said he could even hear the buzzing of flies. He added that the game was "*the* moment. That was the beginning of the current Barcelona model: pressuring high, attacking constantly, pushing the defense into midfield." As soccer authority Jimmy Burns notes, there was a greater significance: "The *New York Times* correspondent later wrote that Cruyff had done more for the spirit of the Catalan nation in 90 minutes than any politicians had achieved in years of stifled struggle."

1975

FC Barcelona v. Real Madrid

El Clásico, December 28, 1975,
Barcelona, Spain

When news of Francisco Franco's death in late November reached Barcelona, a club director happily shattered a bust of the hated dictator against a wall. Catalan jubilation carried over to the meeting of the two rivals several weeks later. As Pete Jenson of *The Independent* notes, "Barça could barely get the Catalan flags (previously banned inside the stadium) sewn fast enough." With hundreds of senyeres fluttering in the stadium, Barcelona jumped out to a quick lead as midfielder Johan Neeskens headed in a goal off a corner kick in the third minute. Madrid evened the score midway through the second half. With time running out, it seemed as though the teams would have to settle for a tie. But a Real defender trying to clear the ball in the 89th minute headed it directly to winger Carles Rexach. His left-footed volley from more than 30 yards out flew into the lower right-hand corner of the net for a 2–1 victory. It wouldn't be Rexach's only significant contribution to the Blaugrana. He is credited with discovering superstar Lionel Messi and signing him to a contract.

1992

FC Barcelona v. Sampdoria

European Cup Final, May 20, 1992,
London, England

The pressure on Barça players to win their first European Cup was almost overwhelming, especially after the bitter 1986 loss in Seville to Steaua Bucureşti on penalty kicks. Manager Johan Cruyff urged his team to relax and simply play, but the players were too anxious. Even though Barcelona dominated the action against Italy's Sampdoria, it missed numerous scoring opportunities, especially one late in the game when forward Hristo Stoichkov's point-blank header was swatted away. Regular time ended 0–0 and raised the ugly possibility of a repeat of Seville. But 22 minutes into extra time, Barcelona received a free kick just outside the penalty area. Midfielder Ronald Koeman blasted a shot through a narrow crease in the line of onrushing defenders into the lower left corner of the net. "Every year people call me to ask if I remember it," Koeman said. "How could I ever forget it?" The match left such an impression on Koeman and all the other players that soccer writer Sid Lowe asserts that "no game has ever been so important for the club."

2009

FC Barcelona v. Real Madrid

El Clásico, May 2, 2009, Madrid, Spain

With five La Liga games in the 2008–09 season remaining, Barça held a narrow four-point lead over Madrid. Madrid had won every game since late December—except for a single tie. A win at home would put the two teams into a virtual tie at the top. Striker Gonzalo Higuaín gave Madrid an early lead, but forward Thierry Henry (pictured, with Messi) quickly evened the score, and defender Carles Puyol gave Barça the lead moments later. Forward Lionel Messi extended the lead to 3–1 shortly before halftime. Though defender Sergio Ramos brought Madrid to within one point early in the second half, Henry quickly restored the two-goal lead. Messi iced the game at the 75-minute mark, and center-back Gerard Piqué completed the rout 8 minutes later. The referee ended one of history's most one-sided El Clásico games after just five seconds of extra time, and Barcelona's 6–2

win halted Madrid's momentum. Eleven days later, Barça won the Copa del Rey and clinched La Liga three days after that. On May 27, the Blaugrana defeated Manchester United 2–0 for the Champions League title and the first-ever Spanish Continental Treble.

FAMOUS FOOTBALLERS

PAULINO ALCÁNTARA

(1896–1964)
Striker, 1912-16, 1918-27

Paulino Alcántara had one of the most spectacular debuts in soccer history, scoring a hat trick for Barça when he was just 15. His career 369 goals was the club's all-time mark until Lionel Messi broke it in 2014. Alcántara played for his parents' native Filipino national soccer and ping-pong teams while living there for two years. But after he fell ill with malaria in 1917, he refused to take any medication unless he could return to Barcelona. According to soccer writer Manel Tomas, "an extraordinarily skinny looking player on the outside was built like a train within, and his ability to strike the ball hard astounded everyone that ever saw him play." This "train build" was evident in 1919 when Alcántara scored the "police goal," a shot so hard that both the ball and a police officer who wandered into its path went sailing into the net. Alcántara retired at the age of 31 to become a doctor and serve on the club's board of directors. In 2007, soccer's international governing body FIFA named him the best Asian player of all time.

FERENC PLATKO

(1898–1983)
Keeper, 1923-30

When Ricardo Zamora left the club, Barça fans didn't believe anyone would be able to take his place. But then Hungarian-born Ferenc Platko stepped in. Perhaps the highlight of Platko's career was in 1928 when he became one of the few soccer players to inspire a poem. In the 1928 Copa del Rey final, an opposing player bore down on Platko. At the last moment, Platko dived for the ball just as the opponent began his kick. He managed to secure the ball but took the full force of the kick on the side of his head. After lying motionless for some time, Platko received six stitches and returned to action with his head bandaged. One of the spectators was poet Rafael Alberti, who was so impressed by Platko's grit and determination that he wrote "Oda a Platko." In the poem, Alberti called Platko the "flaming tiger on the grass of another land" and "blond bear of blood." Platko had a long career as a manager when his playing days were over, including two seasons with Barcelona: 1934–35 and 1955–56.

JOSEP SAMITIER

(1902–72)
Midfielder, 1919–32

Just as New York City's Yankee Stadium was known as "The House That Ruth Built," Barcelona's Les Corts stadium could be called "The House That Samitier Built." The centerpiece of the great Barça teams of the 1920s, Samitier attracted so many fans that a new facility had to be built to accommodate them all. He was that rare player who could field any position (except possibly keeper). His skills in ball-handling and dribbling were legendary. As soccer author Jimmy Burns notes, "El Sami was also blessed with an extraordinary ability to defy gravity, not least with his trademark kick while flying through the air—arms and legs splayed—which earned him the nickname 'Lobster Man.'" Off the pitch, he became an important figure in society and often accompanied leading artists and actors to parties. His origins were considerably more modest. When he signed his first contract at the age of 17, his bonus was a three-piece suit and a watch with glowing hands. Six years later, he was the highest-paid player in Spain. Samitier finished his Blaugrana career with 333 goals, 3rd on the team's all-time list.

JOHAN CRUYFF

(1947–)
Attacking midfielder/ forward, 1973–78
Manager, 1988–96

Dutch-born Johan Cruyff finished second behind the legendary Pelé in a 1999 World Player of the Century poll. During his first season with the Blaugrana, he helped Barça take its first La Liga title in 14 years and won a game against Atlético de Madrid with his "phantom goal." Leaping to take a neck-high crossing pass just beyond the far post, he twisted to face away from the goal and back-heeled the ball into the net while still in midair. Cruyff was a major contributor to the Dutch second-place finish in the 1974 World Cup and Barça's Copa del Rey victory in 1978, his final season. He returned as coach 10 years later. The "Dream Team" he assembled won four consecutive league titles and a European Cup. His total of 11 major trophies made him Barça's most successful manager until his protégé Pep Guardiola surpassed him with 14. Cruyff endeared himself to Catalans in 1974 by naming his son Jordi after the region's patron saint and continued to live in Catalonia, even managing its national team from 2009 to 2013.

ENRIQUE "QUINI" CASTRO

(1949–)
Striker, 1980-84

Barça's long pursuit of Quini, one of La Liga's best strikers, paid off in the summer of 1980 when he signed a huge contract. But the following March, he was kidnapped at gunpoint on the eve of a crucial home game with the league leader for first place. Quini's kidnappers called the next day, explaining that their crime was "because a separatist team [Barcelona] can't win the league." They added that they would release their captive after the game. But they didn't, demanding a huge ransom instead. The uncertainty of Quini's fate was a major distraction for the Blaugrana. Some players had to be ordered to play or face stiff penalties. Though Quini was released unharmed after nearly a month, the damage had been done. In six games during his absence, Barça earned just a single point. The club finished fifth but was only four points out of first. Quini seemed little the worse for his ordeal, finishing that season and the next as *pichichi*, the league scoring champion. He also scored twice in the 1981 Copa del Rey final, leading Barça to a 3–1 win.

LIONEL MESSI

(1987–)
Forward, 2003–present

Growing up in Argentina, Lionel Messi was so small that he was nicknamed "The Flea." Yet he consistently outplayed the older boys. "When you saw him you would think: this kid can't play ball," said his youth coach Adrian Coria. "Because he was explosive, he had a command that I had never seen on a football pitch. He's Formula One, a Ferrari." Unfortunately, the Ferrari had a faulty engine. Messi was afflicted with growth hormone deficiency, a rare medical condition that keeps the body from growing. His family couldn't afford the expensive treatment, nor would any local soccer association help out. However, when Messi was 13, Barcelona invited him to a tryout. He was so impressive that the team signed him and paid for his treatments. Messi used his increased size in 2005 to great advantage when he became the youngest-ever Barça player to score a goal in La Liga play (17 years, 10 months, and 7 days). Since then, he has helped Barça win three Champions League titles, six La Ligas, and two Copas del Rey. Through 2014, he had been named the world's best player four times.

43

FC BARCELONA TITLES
THROUGH 2014

EUROPEAN CUP/ CHAMPIONS LEAGUE	SUPERCOPA DE ESPAÑA
Winner	1983
1992	1991
2006	1992
2009	1994
2011	1996
Total: 4	2005
	2006
Runner-up	2009
1961	2010
1986	2011
1994	2013
Total: 3	Total: 11

COPA DEL REY	LA LIGA
1910	1928–29
1912	1944–45
1913	1947–48
1920	1948–49
1922	1951–52
1925	1952–53
1926	1958–59
1928	1959–60
1942	1973–74
1951	1984–85
1952	1990–91
1953	1991–92
1957	1992–93
1959	1993–94
1963	1997–98
1968	1998–99
1971	2004–05
1978	2005–06
1981	2008–09
1983	2009–10
1988	2010–11
1990	2012–13
1997	Total: 22
1998	
2009	
2012	
Total: 26	

SELECTED BIBLIOGRAPHY

Ball, Phil. *Morbo: The Story of Spanish Soccer.* London: WSC Books, 2003.

Burns, Jimmy. *La Roja: How Soccer Conquered Spain and How Spanish Soccer Conquered the World.* New York: Nation Books, 2012.

Fitzpatrick, Richard. *El Clásico: Barcelona v. Real Madrid; Football's Greatest Rivalry.* London: Bloomsbury, 2012.

Lowe, Sid. *Fear and Loathing in La Liga: Barcelona vs. Real Madrid.* London: Yellow Jersey, 2013.

UEFA. *Champions of Europe, 1955–2005: 50 Years of the World's Greatest Club Football; The Best Goals from All 50 Finals.* DVD. Pleasanton, Calif.: Soccer Learning Systems, 2005.

WEBSITES

FC BARCELONA
http://www.fcbarcelona.com
The FC Barcelona website includes game schedules and
results, news, a detailed history, and more.

LA LIGA
http://www.lfp.es/en/
La Liga's site previews upcoming games and notes the results and
statistics of past matches, league history, and more.

Note: Every effort has been made to ensure that the websites listed above are suitable
for children, that they have educational value, and that they contain no inappropriate
material. However, because of the nature of the Internet, it is impossible to guarantee that
these sites will remain active indefinitely or that their contents will not be altered.

INDEX